The K... for Beginners

Essential Guide to Keto Lifestyle with 70 Easy, Fast & Delicious Recipes

David F. Wilson

Anivya Publishing

DISCLAIMER

CONTENTS

Introduction - Overview

The ketogenic diet (often referred to as the Keto diet or Keto lifestyle) has been massively improving health and transforming lives for the better for millions of people every day.

The Keto lifestyle (eating & living Keto), which includes this "cookbook" is well known as first and foremost, a low carb diet but in reality, it is much more a lifestyle change from modern destructive eating habits.

With the Keto lifestyle, you follow what looks like essentially a low carb way to eat. Yet instead of fueling your body with glucose (sugar), which is very destructive to your health, you also eat a majority of healthy fats and moderate proteins, and this makes your body diminish and eliminate your addiction to sugar.

Further, the Keto lifestyle begins to transform your body to run on healthy fats, producing ketones from your liver.

This is a godsend for Diabetics and obese people who should be almost eliminating all forms of sugar from their diet.

In addition, fueling your body on high natural fats, you reduce insulin and sugar issues and this begins to heal your body. All of the recipes in this cookbook are focused on this goal.

Sugar is very toxic even to non-diabetics and your body actually cannot handle more than a few teaspoons of processed sugar a day. The extra is converted into toxins that impact your health and eventually shorten life and the quality of life.

By eating a diet low in carbs (yes you need to eat some), the body creates a condition called Ketosis; this process is designed to convert fat in the liver into energy.

Primitive man was almost always in a state of Ketosis and because of it he (and she) experienced vibrant health.

The goal of a properly maintained Keto lifestyle is to force your body to remain in this state. This is NOT accomplished via starvation but rather a shift to eating the right mix of foods: about 70% healthy fats, 25% proteins and 5% carbs.

This can be achieved with 99% of the recipes herein.

There have been decades of research and experimentation, and the Keto diet was originally created to treat epilepsy and similar neurological conditions (removal of sugar cures many health issues).

Some of the health benefits of the Keto lifestyle include:

- Steady and ongoing fat Loss.

- Weight control even if you are obese (over time).

- Improved HDL /LDL numbers.

- Almost complete elimination of out of control blood sugar (Diabetics pay attention here).

- Insulin leveling and control.

- Increases in muscle mass.

- Energy levels skyrocketing.

- Mental focus and clarity.

- Decreased cravings and reduced hunger.

- Reduced markers for Cancer, heart disease.

If these reasons are not good enough for you to try the Keto lifestyle, then the ease of these recipes, the flavors and the quick preparation will win you over. Finally, you hold in your hands an incredible tool to completely transform your health and wellness.

Best Regards,
David F. Wilson

Section I: Why You Need The Ketogenic Lifestyle

"The Keytogenic lifestyle" has been said to be perhaps one of the best ways to regain control of your overall health and wellness.

The Keto lifestyle may also be one of the best ways for accomplishing weight loss, especially if you have tried other diets but failed.

Originally created as a way to help control epilepsy, it was discovered to be beneficial also for people who should not eat large amounts of sugar in their diets.

Multiple medical studies (over 25 to date) completely support the theory that the Keto diet / lifestyle taps into early genetic markers that work in concert with your body.

Fueling your body with healthy fats instead of sugar was how our earliest ancestors not only survived, but thrived.

Early man (and woman too) was much more physically fit, healthy, lean and strong. Some of our earliest ancestors were said to be at least twice if not three times stronger than our modern counterparts today.

Early man could run for sometimes hours without getting winded, climb trees like monkeys and were adept hunters and gatherers.

In fact, there is plenty of personal evidence that diets consisting predominately of healthy fats, moderate proteins and low carbs are the hallmark of excellent health.

Adopting the Keto lifestyle and utilizing this special master cookbook you really will begin to enjoy some amazing benefits:

Lose mostly fat stores, not lean muscle – Early man was a powerhouse of muscle and power. He or she was kept naturally slender because the ketones used for fuel were part of what fueled real health.

Think about it for a moment: over a million years of evolution came to shape our eating habits. Paleo man would go sometimes a day or two on low carbs and then eat massive amounts of natural fat laden meats.

Manage and improve heart disease - Fats were at the center of this diet for primitive man. Natural (NOT manmade) fats actually heal your heart and can restore cardiovascular health because your body needs them to run properly.

It is only with the advent of modern diets that disease began to explode. Despite the claims made by modern medicine, we are vastly unhealthier compared to our ancestors and real disease is an extension of our modern love for sugar and contaminated pseudo foods that are foisted on us by our society. Fast foods should be called 'death foods' because study after study links processed foods as a precursor to many forms of disease including Diabetes.

Treat cancers of all kinds – The main fuel for cancer, which is very much like a fungus in the body, is sugar. Many studies link a return to natural foods like green teas, large amounts of vitamin C and cannabis oil as curatives, as long as you are completely off of all processed sugars.

The Keto lifestyle - is so effective at helping to improve lives that many diet companies are actually paying bloggers to scare people away from trying it.

Many articles are emerging warning of the dangers, but when you trace the funding back to who is actually publishing these articles, it is almost always big Agribusiness (Agra).

While you must take into consideration your medical condition before attempting any new way of eating, remember that there are lots of big players who have a vested interest in where you spend your money:

- Big Agra

- Big Pharma

- The diet industry

- The snack industry

- The medical profession

This is just to name a few. It is your body and your life. Think very carefully what you want to do before you give it to any of these corporations that do not care about you, but care very much that you eat their "franken foods," take their drugs and eat their toxic laden products. . .

Section II: More Amazing Facts About The Keto Diet & Why It Works Better Than Almost Any Other "Diet"

The diet can also treat / improve many modern illnesses in addition to what we have already discussed:

Alzheimer's – There is new research finding that the coconut oil used in the diet (in many foods if you follow this cookbook) has a powerful impact on the disease and can lessen or even suppress the disease. Use of raw organic coconut oil as an additive to meals is an additional benefit.

Epilepsy / seizures - The ketogenic diet has been clinically proven to slow or even halt seizures. This is a godsend to people who suffer from seizure disorders. This also includes Parkinson's disease and other related motor function issues.

Diabetes – As mentioned before, as a diabetic you need to remove as much sugar from your diet as possible. Running your body on healthy fats and low carbs will suppress the disease to a point where it essentially no longer causes harm to your body. With Diabetes exploding across the world in massive numbers, the Keto lifestyle is one of the best options as a pre-diabetic (will cure this) or a type I or II sufferer.

Fad Diets – Almost no fad diet is good for your health and in the long run can cost you lean muscle mass. You think you are losing weight, but retaining lean muscle mass is very important especially for older people. Most fad diets strip your body of muscle mass. In addition, a vast majority of people who go on these 'yo yo' diets end up slowing their metabolism to a snail's crawl so as soon as you resume eating even partially like you used to, you pack on even more fat as your body reacts to "starvation" to protect itself from another round of fad dieting.

What does science say? The Keto lifestyle flies in the face of traditional diets as they are flawed:

"Some believe that increased fat in the diet is a leading cause of all kinds of health problems, especially heart disease. This is the position maintained by most mainstream health organizations. These organizations generally recommend that people restrict dietary fat to less than 30% of total calories (a low-fat diet).

However, in the past 11 years, an increasing number of studies have been challenging the low-fat dietary approach. Many health professionals now believe that a low-carb diet (higher in fat and protein) is a much better option to treat obesity and other chronic, Western diseases."

Source: https://authoritynutrition.com/23-studies-on-low-carb-and-low-fat-diets/

There are many studies that now reflect this very statement. People are realizing they have been sold a pack of lies designed to keep them on the diet – a junk food rollercoaster for the profits of the big corporations.

Section III: How & Why It Works, Side Effects And Precautions

Understanding the benefits of the Keto Lifestyle is just part of the picture. We need to review critical information on what makes the Keto lifestyle really work and of course what can derail your progress or even potentially cause you harm.

First of all, understand what you are doing to your body when you start to follow this cookbook and the Keto way of eating:

"Ketosis occurs when people eat a low- or no-carb diet and molecules called ketones build up in their bloodstream. Low carbohydrate levels cause blood sugar levels to drop and the body begins breaking down fat to use as energy. Ketosis is actually a mild form of ketoacidosis."

The Keto diet initially was created by a brilliant Italian doctor called Gianfranco Cappello, an associate professor of surgery at the Sapienza University in Italy (Rome).

The mainstream medical community was in denial for many years concerning his research. It has taken years of irrefutable documented proof in the form of peer-reviewed white papers to finally shut up the medical community, which is now beginning to follow and recreate some of his research.

If you are diabetic or have issues with your blood sugar, the health damage you sustain must be halted at all costs.

Switching to the Keto Lifestyle should always be accompanied by a visit to your current physician, but always keep in mind: doctors today receive almost NO education in nutrition and are trained to write prescriptions.

It is in the best interest of big pharmaceutical companies to keep people like you sick.

Precautions & Side Effects

There is no perfect "diet." In fact, depriving yourself of food you want to eat causes psychological stressors that lead to depression. What you need to do is to finally understand how to fall in love with real whole foods and eat like your ancestors did.

When you first start the Keto Lifestyle, remember you are essentially "detoxing" from the crap foods you have been eating. This is why you should gradually ease into the lifestyle by substitution of each meal over time. For example, start eating Keto breakfasts for a week. Then add Keto snacks for a week. Finally add dinner meals.

Even if you do this carefully, shifting from a mostly sugar diet (which is very toxic) is like a drug abuser getting over his or her addiction. Never go "cold turkey" and switch 100% to Keto eating right away; take it in steps. If you are on medications, you must remember eating this way will heal your body over time and you may not need them anymore.

Diabetics who switch to this way of eating will no longer need insulin, or at least not in the amounts they did before.

This is why you MUST include a physician in the plan to help you. Watch your blood sugar like a hawk and do not use the sliding scale unless approved by a doctor. Eat FIRST, wait one hour and check blood sugar again to make sure how much insulin you need, and when on the Keto diet, NEVER take insulin first.

Remember the elimination of sugar in your diet will reduce all kinds of health issues, including excess weight and higher blood sugar, so you may no longer need your meds, or at least not as much, so watch this carefully and with the help of a physician.

Ketogenic diet will help you lose weight and begin feeling better both physically and mentally. This keto diet can even reverse some weight-related damage to your body as your metabolism changes and you begin to utilize ketones for energy rather than using glucose.

Side effects of eating Keto:

1. Keto "flu" –Just like an addict, you need time to detox from sugar. The effects are similar but much milder; loss of appetite, some nausea, reduced energy, and reduced performance for exercise, mild digestive issues and mild sleep disorders. This will pass in about a week and some people experience no side effects if they ease into the Keto lifestyle.

2. Sluggishness – This is part of the "Keto Flu" and it can be countered with high quality mineral supplementation. ONLY get vitamins that are organic and derived from plant extracts, NOT synthetic. It is very important you do this because you still need plant minerals for optimum health. Try to get top supplements that top athletes use, NOT over the counter crap sold at most big chain stores, i.e. Youngevity.

3. Exercise issues – as you adjust to your new lifestyle remember to keep exercising, but reduce it to just the bare minimum, like walking. This gives your body time to adjust and allows you to regain strength and stamina over time.

Try to follow these suggestions, as they will help you quickly adapt and recover. Over the weeks your strength will not only return but you will begin to feel healthier than ever before.

Now that you understand everything you need to know about the Keto Lifestyle, congratulations!

We are now going to explore some of the best meals you can make quickly. Many of our recipes in this amazing cookbook are easy to prepare and can be made from some of the most common and easy to acquire foods available at your local grocery store.

Always try to get the most organic versions of the ingredients listed and avoid GMO versions. Remember part of the Keto Lifestyle is to detox naturally, so avoid any and all processed foods. Let's get started with really awesome breakfasts, then lunch/dinners and snacks. Enjoy...

Keto Recipes To Start The Day:

Breakfast / Brunch

Breakfast when eating a Keto diet, is a much more balanced way to start the day. Over the next thirty recipes, we will explore some of the very best dishes that both Keto dieticians and experts have been using with their students.

The foods chosen were done with several things in mind:

- Ease of preparation with easy to get ingredients.

- Make most recipes in less than 5 minutes.

- Healthy and affordable ingredients.

It is important to buy the best natural sources of organic, free range and hormone / pesticide free food sources from places like farmer's markets, co-ops and or whole food distributors. Try to avoid big chain stores and focus on locally produced foods.

1. "Monster" Keto Omelet With Avocados

This powerhouse breakfast will not only amaze your taste buds, it is a 'quick build.' Try spice variants like garlic and you will love this great start to the day:

Ingredients:

- ✓ 3 large eggs, whisked together with a dash of salt and pepper

- ✓ 1 diced green pepper

- ✓ ½ sliced avocado, cut in thin strips

- ✓ 2 slices organic bacon, cooked & crumbled

- ✓ ½ small red onion thoroughly diced

- ✓ 1 cup fresh baby spinach

- ✓ 2 tablespoons of avocado oil

- ✓ ¼ cup mild cheddar cheese

- ✓ ¼ cup sour cream

- ✓ Optional spices like garlic, turmeric, basil

Directions:

In a small saucepan, combine one tablespoon of avocado oil with the diced greens, crumbled bacon, sour cream, spinach leaves, and onion. Cook for 2 minutes on a medium heat and remove it from the heat.

In an egg pan (small non-stick fry pan for eggs) add one tablespoon avocado oil. Add eggs in whisked form. Cook on a medium low heat until eggs solidify. Flip and cook on the other side.

Place omelet round on a plate and add the cheddar cheese. Now add all the remaining ingredients to one side of the omelet round. Fold over and garnish with remaining cheese and avocado slices. This delicious omelet will fill you up for most of the day!

2. Coconut Egg Scramble With Rosemary & Thyme

No, this is not a song lyric ("parsley, sage rosemary & thyme"), but when you are finished eating this scramble, you just might feel like singing! The coconut oil and the herbs make this a delicious morning scramble to eat on the fly. Try all of these same ingredients in a low carb veggie wrap to make the meal portable.

Ingredients:

- ✓ 3 eggs, whisked and a dash of salt and pepper added

- ✓ 2 tablespoons grass fed butter

- ✓ 2 tablespoons coconut oil

- ✓ 1 teaspoon rosemary

- ✓ 1 teaspoon thyme

- ✓ ¼ cup diced organic bacon

- ✓ ½ cup diced kale or spinach leaves

- ✓ ¼ cup organic feta cheese

- ✓ 2 veggie wraps

Directions:

In a medium fry pan, combine all ingredients except the feta cheese and the wraps and cook on a medium heat, folding the mix.

As the scramble reduces, fold at a steady speed.

Add the finished mix to a plate and add the feta cheese.

You can also make two wraps out of the ingredients, splitting the feta cheese between the wraps and dividing the ingredients evenly.

3. Sweet & Sassy Keto Breakfast Pork Patties

If you like breakfast patties, this is a great option because you make them yourself. This will also be used in later recipes (as an option). Try these delicious patties but make sure you use free range pork.

Ingredients:

- ✓ 2 pounds pork, free range

- ✓ 1 lime, fresh squeezed

- ✓ 1 teaspoon sage

- ✓ ½ cup coconut oil

- ✓ 1 teaspoon Stevia (plant extract, sweetener, natural)

- ✓ 1 teaspoon maple extract

- ✓ dash of cayenne pepper

- ✓ salt and pepper to taste (several dashes)

Directions:

In a large prep bowl, place the pork and let stand

for 30 minutes with the juice of one lime. Mix and let stand.

Now add all the other ingredients and mix thoroughly.

Preheat oven to 350 degrees. Make round patties from the ingredients, about a 3" diameter (small hockey puck size).

The recipe makes about 6-8 patties. They are flavorful and tangy as well as a healthy version of Keto meat.

4. Keto Zucchini & Coconut Flaked Scrambled Eggs

This delicious and savory variant of a classic breakfast will have you eating your veggies and loving them. Best of all, they are low carbs; just what you would expect from a brilliant Keto lifestyle.

Ingredients:

- ✓ 3 eggs, whisked together with salt and pepper (dash of each)

- ✓ 1 medium zucchini, finely diced (small cubes ¼ inch is best)

- ✓ 2 slices of crumbled organic bacon

- ✓ ½ small white onion

- ✓ 1 clove garlic, diced

- ✓ ½ cup organic coconut flakes

- ✓ 2 tablespoons coconut oil

- ✓ 1 tbsp freshly chopped parsley

Directions:

In a medium frypan, add both tablespoons of coconut oil, the clove of garlic, the onion and the zucchini. Cook on a low heat until the veggies soften, about 2-3 minutes.

Now add the eggs and scramble on a low heat for 5 minutes or until the eggs are cooked.

Add the remaining ingredients for an additional 1 minute.

One variant is to add the coconut flakes last after everything else is cooked with a touch of maple syrup extract.

5. Avocado Barbecue Breakfast Salmon With Eggs

Fish, especially salmon is very good for you. Make sure you source quality wild salmon from places like Alaska, and not farm raised from large chain stores. This dish is a good alternative for brunch while still holding onto eggs for a splash of breakfast taste.

Ingredients:

- ✓ 3 eggs, free range if possible

- ✓ ½ avocado, sliced in strips

- ✓ 2 fillets of salmon medium size

- ✓ 2 tablespoons full fat cream cheese

- ✓ 2 tablespoons of coconut oil

- ✓ 2 tablespoons chopped chives

- ✓ 1 medium spring onion

- ✓ 2 teaspoons butter (organic, real butter only)

- ✓ dash of salt and pepper

✓ 1 cup spinach leaves

✓ 1 cup grated parmesan cheese

✓ 2 teaspoons barbecue seasoning

Directions:

Heat skillet on medium heat, salt and pepper thawed fillets and place on skillet with two tablespoons of coconut oil. Cook on one side until firm and sprinkle the barbecue seasoning on the fish and cook for another minute. Remove patties and add the rest of the ingredients into the same pan and cook on a medium heat until done. Pour the other ingredients over the fish and serve immediately.

6. Zucchini Nests With Bacon, Egg & Cheese

This delicious variant will surprise you as to how good it is. The zucchini becomes more like hash browns and the final product is tasty and fun to make while being fully Keto.

Ingredients:

- ✓ 1 zucchini, peeled & shredded into thin strips similar to spaghetti

- ✓ 4 eggs, whisked together with a dash of salt & pepper

- ✓ 6 strips of organic bacon (raw) cut into strips (thin)

- ✓ ½ cup grated Asiago cheese

- ✓ ¼ cup coconut oil

- ✓ 1 avocado peeled, diced into small cubes

- ✓ ¼ cup parmesan cheese

- ✓ 1 teaspoon basil

- ✓ 1 pinch of salt for each zucchini nest

✓ 1 teaspoon turmeric

Directions:

Take the thin strips of zucchini and spin with a fork like you would do with spaghetti if you were about to eat it. Make small "nests" about 1 inch high.

Place the nests on a flat cookie sheet and drizzle coconut oil through the nest, dividing the ¼ cup of coconut oil among them.

Now add bacon and avocado to the nests. Sprinkle the remaining ingredients over the nests and finally pour the eggs over each nest. Cook in the oven for 20 minutes on 350 degrees.

7. Mushrooms & Egg Scramble With Notes Of Orange

This Keto recipe was given to me by a lady in her 80s. She didn't know it was Keto, but I sure did. This is a flavorful and tasty new experience and will leave you happy and filled.

Ingredients:

- ✓ 4 eggs whisked with a dash of salt and pepper

- ✓ 6 slices of organic bacon, sliced in thirds

- ✓ 2 cups of organic white mushrooms, sliced

- ✓ ½ of a large orange, juiced

- ✓ ½ tablespoon fresh orange zest

- ✓ 1 tablespoon coconut oil

- ✓ ¼ cup heavy whipping cream

Directions:

Cook bacon until crisp, set aside. In a fry pan on a medium heat add mushrooms with scallions and coconut oil and cook for several minutes. Now add the egg mix and scramble.

Just as the eggs are almost done, add all remaining ingredients. It is important that you follow this step for the right consistency and flavor.

Once the scramble is consistent, finish on a medium flame and set aside for a few minutes to let the ingredients set properly.

Variant:

Add salsa and remove the whipping cream.

8. Simple Eggs With Portobello Mushrooms

Here we have a smaller version similar to the last recipe, which is easier to make. This makes a quick breakfast and still keeps you in the Keto zone:

Ingredients:

- ✓ 2 large eggs, cooked over easy in a teaspoon of coconut oil

- ✓ 1 Sweet & Sassy Keto Breakfast Pork Patties (see recipe 3)

- ✓ 2 large Portobello mushrooms diced

- ✓ ½ avocado diced

- ✓ 2 cups spinach leaves

- ✓ 1 tablespoon coconut oil

- ✓ ½ cup salsa, mild or to taste

Directions:

As mentioned earlier, now that you can make Keto sausage patties, we would explore using them in other recipes. If you prefer a variant, skip the patties and use 4 strips of organic bacon.

Crumble the Keto patties (or bacon substitute) on a plate over the spinach. Set aside.

Now cook the mushrooms in a small fry pan with the coconut oil. Cook for several minutes until tender. Add salt and pepper and add to the plate.

Finally cook the eggs and place on top of the ingredients on the plate and add salsa.

9. Feta Peppered Greek Eggs & Tomatoes

Many people on the Keto lifestyle grow to live this flavor so much, it becomes a staple. You will love it too and once you try it you may never feel the same way about Greek eats (unless you already love it).

Ingredients:

- ✓ 4 eggs whisked together with a dash of salt

- ✓ 4-6 oz pre-cooked lamb (optional)

- ✓ 1 teaspoon organic black ground pepper

- ✓ ½ small white onion thoroughly diced

- ✓ ½ cup Feta cheese

- ✓ 1 tablespoon coconut oil

- ✓ ½ clove of garlic, minced

- ✓ ½ cup of cherry tomatoes

- ✓ 2 strips of organic bacon, cooked and crumbled

- ✓ 1 tablespoon of organic Greek salad

dressing to taste

Directions:

In a fry pan, add coconut oil and onion, clove of garlic and the pepper. Cook on a medium heat for about 2 minutes.

Now add the bacon and egg mix and scramble, folding the mix often.

Place cooked eggs on a plate and garnish with the Feta cheese and tomato.

To really get your "Greek" on, add the salad dressing. Also, some people like to add some lamb with their eggs as well.

10. Almond Breakfast Muffins

These muffins are not only delicious but portable, Keto approved and they make great snacks as well as a good meal for breakfast. Mix 'em together and do a quick bake for a dozen of these beauties:

Ingredients:

- ✓ 1¼ cups blanched almond flour

- ✓ ½ teaspoon Himalayan sea salt or plain sea salt

- ✓ ½ teaspoon baking soda

- ✓ 3 eggs

- ✓ ¼ cup almond slivers

- ✓ 2 tablespoons coconut oil

- ✓ 1 tablespoon coconut oil for greasing cupcake tray

- ✓ 1 tablespoon coconut flakes

- ✓ 6 strips organic bacon crumbled

- ✓ 1 cup grated parmesan cheese

- ✓ 2 teaspoons Stevia

- ✓ teaspoon vanilla

Directions:

In a medium mixing bowl, pre-sift blanched almond flour until even consistency. Add eggs first and then vanilla; give about 30 strokes with a large spoon and add almond slivers, coconut oil, stevia and coconut flakes.

In a coconut oil greased cupcake pan, scoop about two tablespoons of batter and bake at 350 for about 15 minutes.

Garnish with crumbled bacon just as they come out of the oven.

11. Power Berry Vanilla Keto Pancakes

Yes, you can have pancakes on the Keto lifestyle, if you make them like this. Once you add the berries, and top them with the whipping cream, you are golden.

Ingredients:

- ✓ 4 egg yolks

- ✓ 1 ½ cups of cottage cheese

- ✓ 1 tablespoon of unbleached flour

- ✓ 1 tablespoon almond flour

- ✓ 2 tablespoons of coconut oil

- ✓ 1 teaspoon vanilla extract

- ✓ 1 cup blackberries

Topping:

- ✓ ¼ cup raspberries

- ✓ 1 cup heavy whipping cream

- ✓ 1 teaspoon Stevia

Directions:

In a mixing bowl add all the ingredients and mix with about 20 strokes. Do not over mix.

Cook on a hot skillet using coconut oil until it bubbles on the sides and flip. Cook until golden brown. Mix topping together and top.

12. Keto Coconut Porridge With Sweet Crème

Many of us still love a good bowl of porridge. Unfortunately, it can be high in carbs. Well, worry no more! Try this and enjoy that hearty flavor. Add fruit and a bit of heavy whipping cream with a touch of Stevia and you are golden!

Ingredients:

- ✓ 2 ½ tablespoons coconut flour, sifted if possible

- ✓ 2 tablespoons flax meal or psyllium husks

- ✓ ¾ cup water

- ✓ 1 egg whisked until even consistency

- ✓ 2 teaspoons natural butter (preferred) or 2 tablespoons coconut oil

- ✓ 1 tablespoon heavy cream or coconut milk

- ✓ 1 teaspoon Stevia

- ✓ ¼ cup favorite berries (suggest blueberries)

Directions:

In a medium saucepan add the coconut flour, flax meal (or psyllium husks) and water. Heat on a low heat until it begins to simmer.

Now add butter (or coconut oil) and slowly whisk in the egg over about a minute (this will incorporate the egg without scrambling it).

Finally add Stevia to heavy whipping cream and the fruit of your choice. Raspberries are also a good variant so try this.

Stevia is a good natural sweetener that also has health properties. Do not use any other sweetener.

13. Mushroom Omelet With Pork Sausage & Spices

One of the best, tasty omelets is a medley of spices with Keto sausage. You have to try this as it took quite some time and experimentation to get the flavors just right.

Ingredients:

- ✓ 3 eggs whisked with a dash of salt and pepper

- ✓ 2 tablespoons of coconut oil

- ✓ ¼ cup shredded cheddar cheese

- ✓ ½ small white onion diced thoroughly

- ✓ 1 Keto pork sausage, (recipe 3 in this guide) crumbled

- ✓ 1 cup diced mushrooms

- ✓ ½ clove of garlic minced

- ✓ 1 teaspoon rosemary

- ✓ 1 teaspoon basil

- ✓ 1 teaspoon allspice

✓ 1 teaspoon sage

Directions:

This recipe is simple. In a fry pan add 1 tablespoon of coconut oil, the garlic, the mushrooms and the allspice. Cook on medium heat for about 3 minutes and set aside.

Next add the crumbled keto pork sausage to the fry pan and cook for about 1 minute on a medium heat. Now add the eggs, mushrooms and the rosemary, basil and sage.

Cook until firm, flip and finish using remaining coconut oil.

14. Seafood Omelet

Believe it or not, having seafood for breakfast is a good way to get going in the morning. Not only will you be getting protein you need, but plenty of Omega 3s too, -- just what the doctor ordered.

Ingredients:

- ✓ ½ package (about 6 oz.) of pre-cooked seafood like shrimp or crab

- ✓ 2 tablespoons olive oil

- ✓ 3 eggs, whisked with a dash of salt and pepper

- ✓ ½ green pepper, diced

- ✓ 1 clove of garlic, minced

- ✓ 1 tablespoon natural butter

- ✓ ½ tablespoon flax seeds

- ✓ ½ tablespoon diced chives

- ✓ 3 strips of organic bacon, cooked & crumbled

- ✓ 3 tablespoons olive oil-based mayonnaise

Directions:

In a flat pan or skillet, heat bacon, cook and crumble. Leave fat from bacon in pan and add the natural butter.

Now cook the eggs in the flat pan, flipping the omelet base on both sides. Remove to a plate ready to receive the other ingredients.

Now add seafood, garlic, green pepper and chives. Cook on a low heat for several minutes stirring frequently.

Add the finished seafood mix to a prep bowl and add mayonnaise, flax seeds and bacon. Mix for about 20 strokes with a large spoon.

Dish out mixture on omelet round and fold in half.

15. Keto Cheese N' Sausage Breakfast Omelet

This delicious omelet was revealed to me while traveling on Route 66. It was intended to be a Paleo breakfast, but when you add more healthy fats and some new spices, it is simply delicious.

Ingredients:

- ✓ 3 eggs whisked with a dash of salt and pepper

- ✓ 2 tablespoons of coconut oil

- ✓ 1 Keto pork sausage, (recipe 3 in this guide) crumbled

- ✓ 3 strips of bacon, cooked & crumbled organic plus the fat from cooking

- ✓ ¼ cup shredded cheddar cheese

- ✓ ¼ cup mozzarella cheese

- ✓ 2 tablespoons parmesan cheese

- ✓ 1 chive, diced

- ✓ 1 teaspoon allspice

✓ 1 teaspoon garlic powder

Directions:

Using one tablespoon of coconut oil, heat a medium omelet skillet and add egg mix cooking on a medium heat.

Flip omelet round and finish cooking and set on a plate.

Now add remaining ingredients into the same pan and cook on a low heat (important to use low heat) for about two minutes.

Add contents from the pan to the plate and fold in half and serve immediately.

16. Keto Bacon & Egg Spinach Cupcakes

Bacon cupcakes? Think them as mini "bread" filled with Keto goodness. Not only are these tasty, but they are easy to bring with you for later meals or snacks on the fly.

Ingredients:

- ✓ 8 eggs whisked with a dash of salt and pepper

- ✓ 4 tablespoons of coconut oil

- ✓ 1 tablespoon olive oil

- ✓ 1 teaspoon baking powder

- ✓ 1 cup spinach leaves fresh, chopped

- ✓ ½ cup sharp cheddar cheese

- ✓ 12 strips of organic bacon, cooked and crumbled

- ✓ 1½ cups almond flour

- ✓ 1 tablespoon sun dried tomatoes, diced

- ✓ 1 clove of garlic minced

✓ 1 teaspoon Stevia

Directions:

Grease a cupcake cooking tray with coconut oil and set aside.

In a large mixing bowl combine all of the dry ingredients plus the bacon, spinach and tomato.

Mix thoroughly and add coconut oil, olive oil, cheese and garlic. Mix until incorporated fully and then start spooning about a tablespoon for each cupcake slot in the baking pan.

Cook at 350 for 15 minutes.

17. Very Berry Cool Keto Crapes

If you love crepes but thought you couldn't have them on the Keto lifestyle, think again. Not only are these super tasty but are some the healthy crepes you can make. So, go ahead and splurge. Keto also means delicious food!

Ingredients:

- ✓ The Crepe batter – (use coconut oil to cook)

- ✓ ½ packet of cream cheese, organic if possible

- ✓ 3 eggs, whisked with a dash of just salt

- ✓ 2 tablespoons almond flower

- ✓ 1 teaspoon Stevia

- ✓ 1 teaspoon cinnamon

- ✓ 1 teaspoon baking soda

- ✓ ½ teaspoon vanilla extract

Filling – (mix in a separate bowl and add to crepes, rolling)

- ✓ ½ package of cream cheese (the other half)

- ✓ ¼ cup blackberries, organic

- ✓ ¼ cup raspberries, organic

- ✓ dash of salt

- ✓ ½ teaspoon vanilla extract

Directions:

Mix all ingredients for the crepes first. Stir for about 30 beats until it runs like maple syrup. Heat the skillet until a drop of water dances on the surface. Cook about a tablespoon of batter quickly on a medium heat, flipping as soon as it bubbles on the edges. Cook until slightly brown and rubbery.

Now add 2 tablespoons of filling and roll like open burritos and serve.

18. Egg Bake With Berries

Egg bakes are simple. Just add the ingredients into a skillet and bake, -- perfect for a quick breakfast. Some people even cook these ahead of time or prepare the bake and pop it in the oven when they are ready.

Ingredients:

- ✓ 6 eggs partially whisked (10 strokes) with a dash of salt and pepper

- ✓ 2 tablespoons natural butter

- ✓ 1 tablespoon coconut oil

- ✓ 3 tablespoons coconut flower

- ✓ ½ teaspoon vanilla extract

- ✓ 1 teaspoon orange zest

- ✓ 1 sprig (small) parsley minced

- ✓ ½ cup berries of your choice

- ✓ 1 teaspoon rosemary, minced

- ✓ ½ teaspoon Stevia (add last as instructed)

Directions:

Preheat oven to 350 degrees.

In a small crock / huge ramekin or Pyrex baking dish with a lid, place butter first and then ½ of the egg mix.

Partially cook eggs first for several minutes and add a dash of salt and pepper again.

Remove from oven for just a moment and add everything else.

Gently stir the bake and add berries last. Sprinkle dash of Stevia last and add the remaining eggs and stir. Cook for 10 minutes and serve.

19. Poached Eggs With Keto Sauce On Spinach

Even though this recipe sounds hard to make, it really isn't. This is a real treat, and if you are having company for breakfast, I would serve this.

Ingredients:

- ✓ 1 hot water egg poacher (or hand poach)

- ✓ 2 eggs, used in the poacher for poaching

- ✓ 1 cup spinach leaves, fresh and cut into a bed of strips

- ✓ 2 slices of bacon, organic pre-cooked

- ✓ 2 slices of fat ham (cut from a shank if possible) precooked.

- ✓ "Hollandaise" Keto Sauce:

- ✓ 2 egg yolks

- ✓ ½ tsp Dijon mustard

- ✓ 2 tablespoons of fresh squeezed lemon juice

- ✓ ¼ cup extra virgin olive oil

- ✓ 1 tablespoon hot water as needed to thin out the mix

- ✓ 1 tablespoon Sriracha sauce (or make your own here)

- ✓ dash salt & pepper to taste

Directions:

Poach eggs as directed and place on a plate over the bed of spinach and on top of the ham.

In a small saucepan, mix all of the sauce over a LOW heat and constantly and gently whisk for about 5 minutes, with less heat and time as the sauce thickens. Pour the mix over the eggs and serve immediately.

20. Keto Cereal And / Or Keto Breakfast Bars

Wow! Now you can have that super crunchy and sweet, satisfying cereal or breakfast bar in the morning or anytime. This recipe can be made and used anytime you crave a sweet & crunchy breakfast treat; only you will know it is low in carbs and almost zero sugar and perfectly nutritious.

Ingredients:

- ✓ ½ cup slivered almonds

- ✓ ¼ cup walnuts

- ✓ 2 tablespoons of coconut oil

- ✓ 1 tablespoon of coconut flakes

- ✓ 2 tablespoons of chia seeds

- ✓ 1 tablespoon of flax seeds

- ✓ 1 teaspoon Stevia

- ✓ 1 tablespoon of coconut flour

- ✓ 1 cup almond milk

Directions:

Mix all of the nuts / seeds with the coconut oil and add coconut flour. Mix completely and then add the remaining ingredients except the almond milk, which you will add when ready to eat as cereal.

Alternate Breakfast Bar without the almond milk:

•   1 teaspoon of cinnamon to the above recipe.

At this point you can also add the ingredients to a small baking pan and bake for 30 minutes on 350. Makes about 3 breakfast bars.

21. Flaxseed, Cinnamon & Egg Fiber Breakfast Muffins

As you may know, flaxseed is very healthy for you. Muffins with flaxseed and other natural additives can heal your body and they actually taste great. Try this recipe and you will also be more regular (if you know what I mean).

Ingredients:

- ✓ 3 eggs, whisked together with a dash of salt

- ✓ 2 tablespoons psyllium husks

- ✓ ¼ cup coconut or almond flour

- ✓ 2 tablespoons of coconut oil

- ✓ 1 cup flaxseeds ground

- ✓ 2 teaspoons Stevia

- ✓ ½ teaspoon baking powder

- ✓ 1 teaspoon cinnamon

- ✓ 1 teaspoon vanilla extract

- ✓ 2 teaspoons almond milk

Directions:

In a medium mixing bowl, place all dry ingredients and dry mix until fully incorporated (well mixed).

Now add all the wet ingredients and beat with a wooden spoon for about 30 strokes.

Preheat oven to 350 degrees. Grease a cupcake baking tin and spoon about 1 well-rounded tablespoon into the cupcake wells.

Cook for 15 minutes or until a toothpick comes out clean from the center of one of the cupcakes.

22. Keto English Muffins For Breakfast Or Anytime

Never thought you could have English muffins again? Think again. These simple 1-minute English muffins taste almost like the real McCoy. These are simple to make and once toasted, crisp on the outside and soft on the inside.

Ingredients:

- ✓ 1 tablespoon of unsalted natural butter
- ✓ 2 tablespoons of almond butter
- ✓ 2 tablespoons of almond or coconut flour
- ✓ ½ teaspoon baking powder
- ✓ 1 tablespoon unsweetened almond milk
- ✓ 1 egg with a dash of salt
- ✓ 1 tablespoon almond milk

Directions:

In a medium mixing bowl, microwave the first two ingredients (natural butter & almond butter) for 30 seconds on high. Stir until it runs smooth. Set aside.

In another mixing bowl, add the flour, baking flour and a dash of salt. Next add the almond milk and the egg and whisk thoroughly. Take the first bowl and add it to the second. Fully incorporate the two together. The final consistency should run like warm syrup.

Split the mix into two medium English muffin size ramekins (small, round microwave safe mini bowls) and microwave each for one minute on high until spongy. You can now remove the "hockey puck" and cut in half and toast just like English muffins / bread!

23. Bacon Egg, Cheese & Coconut Crusted Ham, English Muffins

It is a mouthful to say but once you taste it, you will love this delicious breakfast sandwich. The crusted ham makes sure you get the additional high-quality fats.

Ingredients:

- ✓ 1 Keto English muffin, toasted (see recipe 22)

- ✓ 2 tablespoons of coconut oil

- ✓ 1 tablespoon coconut flakes, unsweetened

- ✓ ¼ cup coconut flakes unsweetened

- ✓ 1 slice of ham, lightly salted and diced

- ✓ 1 egg barely scrambled

- ✓ 1 thin slice sharp cheddar

- ✓ 2 strips of cooked bacon, organic

Directions:

Place one half of the English muffin on a plate and add the cheddar slice. Microwave for ten seconds and then set aside.

Now add one tablespoon of coconut oil to a small fry pan and partially scramble egg leaving it in mostly intact (do not over scramble but cook it thoroughly so it won't fall apart on the sandwich).

In the same fry pan, place 1 tablespoon of coconut oil, the coconut flakes and the slice of ham. Cook both sides, stirring until the oil absorbs most of the coconut oil. Place bacon on top of the cheese, followed by the coconut encrusted ham and the egg. Serve immediately.

24. Perfect Scrambled Eggs & Sausage With English Muffin

This classic breakfast has been made perfect by Keto recipes that combine other flavorful scrambles. You will love this combination so much it just might become your favorite.

Ingredients:

- ✓ 1 Keto sausage (recipe 3)

- ✓ 1 Keto English muffin toasted & buttered (see recipe 22)

- ✓ 1 tablespoon coconut oil

- ✓ 5 eggs, whisked with a dash of salt and pepper

- ✓ 2 tablespoons of natural, salt free butter

- ✓ 2 tablespoons of sour cream

- ✓ 1 tablespoon diced scallions

- ✓ 4 strips organic bacon

- ✓ ½ teaspoon garlic powder

- ✓ ½ teaspoon onion powder

✓ 1 dash paprika

✓ 1 dash Stevia

Directions:

Add coconut oil to a medium skillet and cook bacon in the oil. Do NOT drain fat and remove bacon. Now add eggs and start cooking for about 1 minute on a medium heat.

Next add all remaining ingredients, including the bacon (crumbled), except the sausage, which you need to heat up last and put on the English muffin.

Fold eggs / remaining ingredients continuously, until the food begins to thicken. Add on top of English muffin and sausage.

25. Mini Keto Quiches With Sun Dried Tomato & Basil

This fun recipe can yield several of these quiches to heat and eat anytime. The flavor will surprise you because eating Keto need not be bland.

Ingredients:

- ✓ 12 eggs, whisked together with 1 teaspoon pepper & ½ teaspoon salt

- ✓ ¼ cup sun dried and crumbled tomatoes, sun dried or dehydrated

- ✓ ¼ teaspoon of cayenne pepper

- ✓ 1 teaspoon tomato paste

- ✓ 1 teaspoon basil

- ✓ ½ cup mozzarella

- ✓ 1 diced jalapeño (optional but adds zing)

- ✓ ½ teaspoon Stevia

- ✓ 1 teaspoon olive oil

- ✓ 1 tablespoon coconut oil

- ✓ 5 strips of bacon cooked & crumbled (add bacon fat as well)

Directions:

Add all ingredients to a mixing bowl and beat for about 30 strokes.

Preheat oven to 350.

Into 2-3 large ramekins or 1 flat pie tin, pour ingredients and bake for for 25 minutes. Allow quiche to cool for 30 minutes or pop in the freezer for 15 minutes.

One variant is to also add ¼ cup of sharp cheddar and the bacon crumbles on the top of the quiche.

26. Ham Egg & 2 Cheese Coconut Fried Rollups

While this might sound fattening, on the Keto you need lots of healthy fats. Using coconut oil to fry these beauties (pan fried) makes them crispy, delicious and even nutritious. So, if you are looking for a real treat, give this a try.

Ingredients:

- ✓ 6 flour torts, (burrito wraps large) low carb or made from coconut flour

- ✓ 12 slices ham, preferably from the shank but slices will do

- ✓ 12 eggs whisked with a dash of salt and pepper

- ✓ 1 tablespoon of coconut oil for cooking eggs

- ✓ 3 cups of baby spinach leaves (1/2 cup per tort)

- ✓ 12 strips of bacon, organic cooked (2 each tort)

- ✓ ½ cup sour cream

- ✓ 3 scallions diced

- ✓ 3 tomatoes, organic diced

- ✓ 3 cups sharp cheddar (1/2 cup each tort)

- ✓ 3 cups Monterey jack cheese (1/2 cup each tort)

- ✓ Pinch of Stevia for topping on torts (each)

- ✓ ½ cup coconut oil for cooking

Directions:

Add a tablespoon of coconut oil in a medium to large skillet and then the eggs. Add the sour cream and more pepper (to taste) plus the scallions, cooking on a medium heat until scrambled. Set aside. Now cook bacon and drain grease in the egg mix. Crumble.

On a tort add everything else (divide ingredients as mentioned for each wrap) and roll tight into a burrito. In a large skillet add coconut oil and fry the burritos on high heat for several minutes on both side and set on paper towels. Garnish with Stevia and serve immediately.

27. Cauliflower Pepper Hash Browns

I know you miss hash browns on the Keto lifestyle, but these are almost as good if you follow the directions. They are also going to be healthy and tasty so you'll never miss out again.

Ingredients:

- ✓ 1 head of cauliflower, shredded with a cheese collider (make strips)

- ✓ 1 cup sharp cheddar

- ✓ 1 egg whisked with dash of pepper & salt

- ✓ ½ teaspoon of black pepper

- ✓ ½ teaspoon white pepper

- ✓ dash of cayenne pepper

- ✓ ¼ cup coconut oil for cooking

Directions:

In a medium mixing bowl, add all ingredients and stir gently until everything is incorporated.

Set aside.

In a medium to large skillet, add coconut oil and heat on high (be careful of heat).

Add 2 tablespoons of the cauliflower mix to a hot skillet and press flat like a pancake. Cook until golden brown on both sides.

You can also add tabasco sauce for a real zing or salsa once the cauliflower is cooked.

28. Cloud Bread For Breakfast / Lunch / Dinner

Many of us grew up on bread. It is very satisfying to eat but has way too many carbs. Well NOT this bread! You only need three ingredients for this but you have to follow the directions carefully . . . so we put everything you need in the ingredients list for ease of understanding.

Ingredients:

- ✓ 3 eggs, separated whites from the yolks

- ✓ 2 medium mixing bowls: one for yolks, the other for the whites

- ✓ 1 cookie tray lined with wax paper

- ✓ 3 tablespoons of cream cheese, at room temperature

- ✓ 1 teaspoon of baking powder

Directions:

Preheat oven to 350 and set up cookie tray with wax paper on it. In the bowl with the yolks (do this first) add the cream cheese and whip on medium high until incorporated completely. Using room temperature cream cheese is critical for this to work right.

Clean mixer beaters in cold water and refrigerate beaters until cold to the touch before going to the egg whites. In the bowl with the egg whites add the baking powder and whip on medium to high until the consistency of Meringue (like cool whip and will stand up on its own).

Carefully fold both bowls of ingredients together preserving as much air as possible. Now add a dollop of the mix on the wax paper the size of the cloud bread that you want. Cook for 10 minutes and then 1 minute on broil to brown the top.

29. Cream Cheese Keto Pancakes With "Whipped Cream" Topping

What could be better for breakfast than pancakes? Well give these a try and you won't believe just how good Keto pancakes can be.

Ingredients:

- ✓ 2 eggs whisked
- ✓ 3 tablespoons cream cheese
- ✓ ½ cup coconut flour
- ✓ 1 dash vanilla extract
- ✓ ½ teaspoon baking powder
- ✓ ½ teaspoon Stevia
- ✓ 1 tablespoon coconut oil
- ✓ ½ teaspoon cinnamon

Topping:

- ✓ ½ cup heavy whipping cream
- ✓ ½ teaspoon line juice

✓ ½ teaspoon Stevia

✓ ½ teaspoon vanilla extract

Directions:

Mix flour and baking powder first, then everything else for about 30 beats with a large wooden spoon. Do not over mix and leave reasonably thick. Heat skillet until a drop of water dances on it and add coconut oil. Add about a tablespoon of batter and cook until golden brown. In a mixing bowl add topping ingredients, blend on high until fluffy and serve on the pancakes.

30. Sausage, Egg & Ham Patty With Breakfast Sandwich

Here is a great combination to round off our final breakfast recipe. Using recipes 3 & 28 will finish this one, recipe 30.

Ingredients:

- ✓ 1 Keto sausage patty (see recipe 3)

- ✓ 2 slices of cloud bread (see recipe 28)

- ✓ ¼ cup sharp cheddar

- ✓ 1 egg

- ✓ ½ tablespoon coconut oil

- ✓ ½ of a medium avocado sliced in wedges

- ✓ 1 slice of ham preferably from a ham shank

Directions:

Prepare the Keto sausage as directed in recipe 3. Prepare the cloud bread as in recipe 28.

Cook the single egg in a small fry pan using the coconut oil and cook on a medium heat. Cook the egg until it is over hard so it won't explode when you bite down in the sandwich.

Next add the cloud bread, the cheese on both slices and microwave for about ten seconds to melt the cheese slightly.

Last add ham & avocado.

Variant: Use the Keto English muffin recipe 22 instead of cloud bread.

Delicious And Easy To Prepare Keto Dinners

This section includes quick and easy dinners / brunches. The idea is to make sure recipes are made of simple ingredients, yet complex enough for real flavor.

We do not include "lunch" because any of the dishes here can be used for that purpose as well because of ease of preparation.

We will start with some great slow cooker meals as they can be put in a crockpot and cooked on low while you are at work or out of the house for a few hours.

We also include complete meals and we are targeting about 4 people. If you want recipes for two people, simply cut the ingredients in half.

If you need to prepare for about 6 people add an additional 1/3 of everything, simple and fast.

Now lunch/dinner can be an experience without all the fuss!

1. Slow Cooker Beef 'n Broccoli For Four

This classic dinner is simple and easy to make. Keto means more natural fats which help your body remain in the correct zone. This meal is great on a cold day and is hearty.

Ingredients:

- ✓ 2 pounds of stock beef cubed for slow cooking

- ✓ 3 cups of water with beef stock (2 cubes)

- ✓ 3 scallions diced

- ✓ 2 teaspoons of Stevia

- ✓ 1 teaspoon fresh ginger

- ✓ ½ teaspoon Himalayan salt and organic ground black pepper

- ✓ 2 tablespoons coconut oil

- ✓ 1 tablespoon olive oil

- ✓ 3 garlic cloves, minced

- ✓ 1 teaspoon sesame seeds

- ✓ 1 teaspoon flax seeds

- ✓ 2 diced bell peppers

- ✓ 2 cups fresh broccoli

- ✓ 1 carrot diced

- ✓ 1 small white onion diced

Directions:

The beautiful thing about slow cooker meals are that everything usually goes into the pot and you set it on low and cook for at least 4-8 hours depending on ingredients. (this recipe is best at 6 hours)

A taste variant is to flash fry the beef with a pinch of Stevia and 1 tablespoon natural butter for additional taste.

2. Double Beef & Veggies Slow Cooker Stew

Slow cooker meals are wonderful for those of us on the move. Now you can add more beef and other veggies because this makes for a heartier meal.

Ingredients:

- ✓ 3 pounds of stock beef cubed for slow cooking

- ✓ 2 cups of water with beef stock (2 cubes)

- ✓ 1 teaspoon fresh ginger

- ✓ ½ teaspoon Himalayan salt and organic ground black pepper

- ✓ 2 tablespoons coconut oil

- ✓ 1 tablespoon olive oil

- ✓ 3 garlic cloves, minced

- ✓ 2 diced bell peppers

- ✓ 2 cups diced cauliflower

- ✓ 2 carrots diced

- ✓ 1 small white onion diced

- ✓ ½ cup of snap peas (uncooked, fresh)

- ✓ 1 tablespoon Worcestershire sauce

Directions:

Add all ingredients into slow cooker and cook on low for 6-8 hours. This is a great meal if you have to go to work. If you want to spice it up add about 1 /2 tablespoon hot sauce.

Another variant is to flash fry with coconut oil, the cubes of beef with a teaspoon of Stevia and garlic (2 cloves crushed).

Finally, a dash of coconut flour as you finish the flash fry carries the flavor into the stew.

3. Cheddar Taquitos With Classic Taco Sauce

Almost everybody loves Mexican cuisine. These simple but delicious taco "rolls" can also be fried with coconut oil to add some crunch and if you serve on a bed of diced tomatoes and romaine lettuce, are out of this world when it comes to flavor.

Ingredients:

- ✓ 1 pound of hamburger, free range

- ✓ 1 taco seasoning packet - try to get Taco Bell™ version if possible

- ✓ 1 cup diced Roma tomatoes

- ✓ 1 avocado cubed

- ✓ 12 small low carb flour torts OR almond / coconut torts

- ✓ 2 cups Mexican cheese (mix / 4 cheeses)

- ✓ 1 cup sour cream

- ✓ 1 cup coconut oil for flash frying of wrapped torts

- ✓ 1 cup salsa, mild (or hot if you prefer)

- ✓ ½ cup mild taco sauce

Directions:

Cook hamburger (do NOT drain fat), and seasoning (packet) and set aside.

Assemble the torts by adding all ingredients so as to divide them among the small torts you have. Roll tight and make sure they are closed (like taquitos).

Heat skillet with coconut oil and fry until golden brown. Serve on a bed of diced tomatoes and romaine lettuce with dipping taco sauce.

4. Keto Pizza Rolls

These simple fried and seasoned "rolls" are a great option to commercially produced toxic pizza rolls often sold in your grocer's freezer.

Ingredients:

- ✓ 5 small low carb torts
- ✓ ½ cup coconut oil
- ✓ ½ cup pepperoni diced
- ✓ 2 cups mozzarella cheese
- ✓ ¼ cup of pizza seasoning
- ✓ ¼ cup white onion minced
- ✓ ½ cup diced green peppers
- ✓ 1 Keto sausage, crumbled (see recipe 3)
- ✓ ½ cup pizza sauce

Directions:

On each tort place an even amount of the ingredients like you would with a burrito. The measurement above should be evenly divided.

Wrap the torts tightly and set aside.

Heat a medium or large skillet with the coconut oil. Heat for about 5 minutes on a medium flame and take 2 torts at a time and flash fry them, turning in the pan until they are golden brown.

Remove torts onto a stack of paper towels and lightly sprinkle with additional pizza seasoning while hot.

One variant is to add hot sauce or jalapenos . . . hot, hot!

5. Keto Broccoli Cheesy Fried Tort Rolls

Similar to the last recipe, this one will make a good plan for dinner and you will have delicious leftovers that can be taken with you on the fly.

Ingredients:

- ✓ 5 large torts, low carb

- ✓ 3 cloves crushed & minced garlic

- ✓ ¼ cup organic true olive oil

- ✓ ¼ cup coconut oil for frying

- ✓ 2 cups shredded mozzarella cheese shredded

- ✓ ½ cup shredded Monterey jack and / or sharp cheddar (mix both)

Broccoli steamed:

- ✓ 2 cups diced / steamed fresh broccoli heads

- ✓ 1 teaspoon lemon pepper

- ✓ 1 tablespoon natural butter

Directions:

First steam broccoli (or heat up on stove with ¼ cup of water) and mix in lemon pepper and butter.

Next add olive oil and both cheeses. Mix well and scoop out enough mix for each burrito, wrapping them tight.

Heat a skillet on medium heat with the coconut oil. Pan fry each burrito until golden brown and serve immediately.

6. Chicken & Pork Ear Super Keto Bake With Veggies

This modified classic chicken bake gets its inspiration from Shake 'n' Bake™. Once you add the cooking oils and use them to bind everything together you will love it.

Ingredients:

- ✓ 2 pounds boneless chicken breasts split into long strips

- ✓ 2 clear plastic bags for shaking chicken with spices

- ✓ 3 cups mixed veggies

- ✓ ½ teaspoon garlic powder

- ✓ ½ teaspoon onion powder

- ✓ ½ cup parmesan cheese

- ✓ ½ tablespoon Italian seasoning

- ✓ ½ teaspoon chicken bouillon (dry)

- ✓ ½ teaspoon chili pepper

- ✓ 2 cups crushed pigs ears

- ✓ 2 eggs whisked with a pinch of salt and pepper

- ✓ ½ cup coconut oil

- ✓ ¼ cup olive oil

Directions:

In a medium mixing bowl add all of the dry ingredients and incorporate everything together. Place dry ingredients in a bag.

Place veggies mixed with the oils on the bottom of a pyrex glass baking dish or lasagna pan.

Dip chicken on egg wash and then place in bag with dry ingredients and shake. Place chicken on a bed of the veggies and bake for 30 minutes, flipping chicken in about 15 minutes.

7. Keto Whipped "Potatoes"

Heavy carbs are a 'no – no' on the Keto lifestyle. Many of us crave potatoes and there is only one way to deal with this craving. . . Keto potatoes to the rescue!

Ingredients:

- ✓ 1 large or 2 medium cauliflower heads, steamed & crumbled

- ✓ ½ tablespoon potato flakes

- ✓ ½ cup whole milk

- ✓ 3 tablespoons natural butter

- ✓ ½ cup heavy cream

- ✓ 1 tablespoon coconut oil

- ✓ ½ teaspoon salt

- ✓ ½ teaspoon garlic salt

- ✓ ¼ teaspoon cracked or white pepper

- ✓ ¼ cup parmesan cheese

Directions:

In a medium mixing bowl add potato flakes and milk and one tablespoon of butter and 1 tablespoon coconut oil. Whip on medium speed for 30 seconds with a hand mixer.

Next add the cauliflower, salt, pepper and remaining 2 tablespoons of butter and whip for another 30 seconds on high.

Finally add heavy cream and parmesan cheese and whip on high for 2 minutes or until it reaches the the consistency of whipped potatoes.

You will still need to heat it up, so either microwave for 3 minutes on high or in a pot on the stove for several minutes on a medium flame stirring several times until everything is thick.

8. Mexican Beef Skillet

This simple recipe looks like it would be difficult but the directions are akin to a tossed salad. Try it and you will make this for dinner more than once.

Ingredients:

- ✓ 2 ripe avocados sliced into strips like potato wedges

- ✓ 1 teaspoon freshly squeezed lime juice

- ✓ 2 chives diced

- ✓ 1 small white onion diced

- ✓ 2 Roma or small cherub tomatoes diced

The Beef:

- ✓ 2 pounds of cubed stew beef

- ✓ 1 beef stock cube

- ✓ 1 tablespoon taco sauce

- ✓ ¼ cup olive oil

- ✓ ½ cup water

Condiments:

- ✓ 2 cups shredded lettuce

- ✓ ½ cup Mexican taco cheese

- ✓ 1 cup sour cream

Directions:

In a large fry pan on medium heat, cook all of the beef ingredients for about 5 minutes and remove from heat and place in a mixing bowl. Add remaining ingredients and gently stir together.

Preheat oven to 350 and place everything in an oven safe skillet and cook for 15 minutes. Serve immediately.

9. Spaghetti & Meat Squash

Do you miss spaghetti? Here is a fun and delicious substitute that will make you think you are eating pasta when you are actually eating veggies.

Ingredients:

- ✓ 2 large Spaghetti squash

- ✓ 2 tablespoons coconut oil

- ✓ 1 pound of grass fed ground beef

- ✓ 1 cup Parmesan cheese

- ✓ 1 teaspoon chili powder

- ✓ 1 teaspoon Italian seasoning

- ✓ ½ teaspoon oregano

- ✓ 2 cloves of garlic, minced

- ✓ 3 cups pasta sauce

- ✓ ¼ cup coconut flour

Directions:

Cook spaghetti squash on 350 for an hour. Gut the squash in long strips (it tends to come out like this).

Add to mixing bowl with coconut flour and coconut oil and gently fold with a spatula until thoroughly mixed.

Next cook beef with all the spices until brown. Do NOT drain fat and add spaghetti sauce.

Finally, place spaghetti squash on the plate first, add parmesan cheese (divide among servings).

Now add spaghetti sauce with meat on top and serve immediately.

You can add pepper flakes or chili spice for more zest.

10. Lebanese Chicken Thighs

Time for something really different with this classic Middle Eastern dish made to be 100% Keto compliant.

Ingredients:

- ✓ 4 chicken thighs with skins intact

- ✓ 2 cups of water

- ✓ 1 chicken bouillon cube

- ✓ ¼ cup garlic olive oil (or add two cloves of garlic to olive oil)

- ✓ 2 tablespoons natural butter

- ✓ 1 white onion quartered (do not dice)

- ✓ 2 carrots diced

- ✓ 2 celery stalks diced

- ✓ 2 small tomatoes cut in quarters

- ✓ 1 lemon juiced

- ✓ ¼ cup soy sauce

- ✓ 3 cups diced lettuce and field greens

Directions:

Preheat oven to 350. Mix all ingredients into a small pyrex dish (with a lid) and mix all ingredients into a mixing bowl and pour over chicken.

Cover the bowl with the lid and cook for 30 minutes.

On a plate, put 2 thighs on about 2 cups of the greens and scoop a cup of the broth from the chicken and pour over it.

One variant is to add parmesan cheese over the greens.

Another variant is to add ½ a cup of olives.

Regardless, you will love the savory flavor so serve immediately.

11. Chicken Kabobs

Who doesn't love kabobs? They can be carried and eaten on a stick and each is a flavorful exploration of the world's best and delicious foods that also happen to be Keto.

Ingredients:

- ✓ 2 pounds of chicken, or lamb cut into kabob chunks

- ✓ 4 wooden skewers, cut veggies of choice to add to kabob.

Feta Marinade:

- ✓ 1 cup of Feta brine

- ✓ ½ cup olive oil

- ✓ ½ tablespoon lemon juice

- ✓ ½ teaspoon rosemary

- ✓ 3 cloves of garlic, minced

Italian Variant:

- ✓ ½ cup olive oil

✓ 1 lime, juiced

✓ ½ teaspoon chili powder

✓ ½ teaspoon onion powder

✓ 3 cloves of garlic, minced

Directions:

In a lasagna pan or rectangular Pyrex dish, place the ingredients for the marinade. Place chicken in dish and let stand for 4 hours at room temperature and for at least 12-24 hours in the refrigerator. When ready, grill for 5 minutes on each side on an outside grill. Make sure internal temperature of chicken reaches 140 degrees.

12. Italian "Breaded" Pork Cutlets

Pork cutlets are a good meal especially if you like them "breaded." Why is breaded in quotes? Well look at the recipe and you will understand.

Ingredients:

- ✓ 6 pork cutlets lightly salted and peppered

- ✓ ½ cup Italian dressing & ½ cup water in medium bowl

- ✓ ½ cup grated parmesan cheese

- ✓ 2 eggs whisked in medium bowl

- ✓ 1 cup crushed pigs ears

- ✓ 1 dash Italian seasoning

- ✓ 1 sprig of parsley

- ✓ ½ cup coconut oil

Directions:

Soak cutlets for 4 hours in Italian dressing and water at room temperature.

Preheat oven to 350 degrees. Dip cutlets in egg

wash and then dip in parmesan and crushed pigs ears with a dash of Italian dressing.

Now place in the Pyrex dish and cover with coconut oil. Bake for 20 minutes.

You can garnish with parsley by dicing and adding on top of cutlets just before they finish cooking. You can also add a dash of applesauce and a touch of cinnamon for more flavor.

13. Keto Pot Roast With Brown Gravy & Mashed "Potatoes"

Pot roast with gravy & mashed potatoes is a staple in America. People love this meal especially on cold days. It reminds us of fall and winter. Try it today and see!

Ingredients:

- ✓ 1 medium pot roast, with "dry rub" applied

- ✓ 2 cups beef broth

- ✓ ½ cup olive oil or garlic olive oil

- ✓ 1 serving of Keto whipped "potatoes" see recipe 7 (Keto Dinners)

Rub:

- ✓ ½ teaspoon thyme

- ✓ ½ teaspoon tsp celery salt

- ✓ 1 teaspoon basil

- ✓ 2 teaspoon dried dill weed

- ✓ 2 teaspoons garlic powder

- ✓ 1 tablespoon oregano

Gravy:

- ✓ 1 cup meat drippings

- ✓ 1 packet brown gravy mix

Preheat oven to 350 degrees. Mix the ingredients for the rub and apply to the pot roast and put in a pot roast pan with a lid.

Cook for one hour and use meat drippings to make gravy. Prepare "potatoes" according to recipe 7 and plate it up. Enjoy!

14. Chicken Soup Bone Broth

Bone broth is actually very healthy for you. Plus, it can be seasoned to taste great. The next time you need a pick me up, try this:

Ingredients:

- ✓ 1 whole chicken medium to large
- ✓ 10 cups of water
- ✓ ½ yellow onion minced
- ✓ 1 tablespoon onion powder
- ✓ 2 tablespoons minced garlic
- ✓ 1 tablespoon garlic salt
- ✓ 1 teaspoon dried thyme
- ✓ 2 cups diced celery
- ✓ 1 tablespoon apple cider vinegar
- ✓ ½ cup coconut oil
- ✓ 2 chicken bouillon cubes

Directions:

In large pot place thawed whole chicken and cover with water, about 10 cups, more or less as needed. Boil for 1 hour and remove from stove. SAVE WATER and filter with a strainer.

Separate the meat and the bones. Pour water back in the same pot and add JUST the large bones. Boil for 20 more minutes. DO NOT micro STRAIN except for any bone fragments.

Add the broth to another pot with the chicken and all the ingredients plus 2 chicken bouillon cubes. Cook on a low heat for 15 minutes.

Serve just like chicken soup. This is very healthy, low carb and nutritious.

15. Chicken Veggie Casserole

This classic dinner is a snap and will also leave you happy and healthier than most dinners. Try this wonderful and flavorful variant and you will love it.

Ingredients:

- ✓ 2 boneless chicken breasts

- ✓ 3 tbsp natural butter

- ✓ 1 small white onion minced

- ✓ ½ tablespoon minced garlic

- ✓ 1 cup chicken stock (or chicken soup bone broth recipe 14-Keto Dinners)

- ✓ 1 pinch of parsley or diced sprig

- ✓ Ingredients for Casserole:

- ✓ 3 cups cauliflower

- ✓ 1 cup heavy cream

- ✓ 1 tsp lemon juice

- ✓ ½ cup mayonnaise

- ✓ 3 cups steamed, chopped broccoli

✓ 2 cups shredded cheddar cheese

Directions:

Place first set of ingredients in a skillet on the stove and cook for about 5 minutes, flipping chicken in about half the time. Set aside.

Preheat oven to 350 degrees and place all casserole ingredients first, then the chicken and the rest on top. Cook for 30 minutes and remove and serve immediately.

16. Best Keto Meatballs On Planet Earth?

Well maybe not The best, but darn close. Try these, but pay close attention to the recipe because if you do you will love these.

Ingredients:

- ✓ 1 lb. ground beef, lamb or pork made / processed like hamburger

- ✓ ½ cup grated parmesan cheese

- ✓ ½ cup olive oil

- ✓ ½ cup ground pigs ears

- ✓ ½ tablespoon barbecue seasoning

- ✓ ½ packet sloppy joe seasoning

- ✓ ½ teaspoon white cracked pepper

- ✓ ½ teaspoon Himalayan salt

- ✓ 1 tablespoon minced garlic

- ✓ ½ cup mozzarella cheese

- ✓ 1 teaspoon onion powder

Directions:

In a medium mixing bowl, place all ingredients and incorporate until the consistency of what you might use for hamburger patties.

Preheat oven to 350 degrees.

On a long cookie sheet roll about 2 tablespoons of the meat & spice mix into balls, about the size of golf balls.

Place on sheet and cook for 15 minutes. You can also turn these into hamburgers by simply changing their shape.

17. Best Hot / Mild Slow Cooker Chicken wings

Many people love wings. The best part is slow cooker recipes, which can add spice to your day and make cooking a snap.

Ingredients:

- ✓ 1 bag of chicken wings, unprocessed

- ✓ ½ stick natural butter (3-4 tablespoons)

- ✓ 1/4 cup hot sauce of choice OR ½ tablespoon paprika (non-hot)

- ✓ 2 cloves of garlic, minced

- ✓ ½ a lime, fresh squeezed

- ✓ If you like honey add these ingredients:

- ✓ ½ cup of natural local honey

- ✓ ½ a lemon, fresh squeezed

If you like Barbecue sauce add these ingredients:

- ✓ 1 tablespoon barbecue spice

✓ ½ tablespoon apple cider vinegar

Directions:

Add the chosen ingredients into a slow cooker and cook on low for 4 hours. Finish on high for 30 minutes and remove. Serve with celery & bleu cheese.

You can also add a side of Keto ranch dressing for flavor.

18. Meat Bacon Tacos

Many people love bacon, so why not make these delicious bacon tacos? Not only these are fun to eat but very flavorful.

Ingredients:

- ✓ 1 pound of hamburger cooked

- ✓ 1 taco seasoning packet OR ¼ cup taco sauce

- ✓ ¼ cup taco sauce for garnish on the tacos

- ✓ ¼ cup ranch dressing

- ✓ 2 cups shredded thinly sliced lettuce

- ✓ ½ cup diced tomatoes

- ✓ 20 strips of bacon

- ✓ 2 eggs whisked

Directions:

On a plastic microwave bacon dish, lay out 5 strips of bacon over the cooking mold to form a "taco shell" or upside down "U." Brush with egg wash and microwave until it forms a shell, about 4 minutes.

Cook hamburger meat and add taco seasoning or taco sauce.

Now add all ingredients to build a taco. This includes dividing all ingredients up among the 4 tacos you will make.

If you do not want all the bacon, you can substitute small torts.

Another possibility is to create a taco bowl out of this by adding the lettuce and diced bacon with all the rest of the ingredients in a small bowl.

Finally add a dash of tabasco sauce for a kick.

19. Philly Cheese Stuffed Coconut Coated Peppers

This is a delicious way to enjoy Philly cheese steak and get all of the good fats. Staying Keto has never been easier.

Ingredients:

- ✓ 4 medium green bell peppers
- ✓ 4 tablespoons of natural butter
- ✓ ½ cup white onion chopped
- ✓ 1 teaspoon minced garlic
- ✓ 1-pound shaved Philly steak
- ✓ 3 tablespoons coconut oil
- ✓ 1 cup Monterey Jack cheese
- ✓ 1 cup mozzarella
- ✓ 1 tablespoon of Italian dressing
- ✓ 2 tablespoons of mayonnaise

Directions:

In a large skillet place the coconut oil, Italian dressing and pre-cook for about 5 minutes. Set aside.

Preheat oven to 350 degrees.

Now cut peppers in half and place in a cooking tray. Mix steak with remaining ingredients.

Add a dash of salt and pepper and bake for 15 minutes.

Add steak sauce for a variant.

20. Lemon Squash "Pasta" With Lamb Or Steak

This veggie dish is filled with good fats and some solid meat too. Lemon pepper makes it all sync together.

Ingredients:

- ✓ 1 pound of lamb or steak cubed

- ✓ 3 yellow summer squash

- ✓ 1 tablespoon lemon pepper seasoning

- ✓ 2 tablespoons olive oil

- ✓ 1 tablespoon coconut oil

- ✓ 2 cloves of garlic minced

- ✓ ¼ cup parsley diced

- ✓ ½ lemon fresh squeezed or juiced

Directions:

Preheat oven to 350 degrees. Cut squash in half and cook for 45 minutes on a cookie sheet.

On the stove pre-cook the meat of choice for

several minutes with all of the ingredients except the squash.

Now add the scooped-out squash to the skillet and fold for about 10 minutes until everything is mixed well.

You can add some salt, but I suggest you skip the pepper.

You can also serve on a bed of romaine and spinach leaves as this flavor is more enhanced by adding some uncooked greens.

An additional variant is to cook a bit more meat for a heartier dinner, -- like 2 pounds instead of one.

21. Keto Meatloaf

A good meatloaf is a joy unto itself. Simply add all ingredients and cook in the oven. In 30 minutes you have a meal for the entire family.

Ingredients:

- ✓ 2 lbs fatty ground beef

- ✓ 2 eggs

- ✓ 1 tablespoon coconut oil

- ✓ 2 tablespoons olive oil

- ✓ 1 tablespoon tomato paste

- ✓ ½ white onion minced

- ✓ ½ teaspoon Himalayan salt

- ✓ 4 cloves garlic minced

- ✓ ½ teaspoon Dijon mustard

- ✓ ½ cup crushed pigs ears

- ✓ ¼ cup parmesan cheese

- ✓ 1 tablespoon Worcestershire sauce

- ✓ ½ cup mozzarella cheese

- ✓ 1 tablespoon barbecue sauce

- ✓ ¼ cup sesame seeds or flax seeds

Directions:

In a large mixing bowl leave meat out for 1 hour to warm it up for ease of handling. Preheat oven to 350 degrees. Place all remaining ingredients and mix by hand. On a cooking sheet form the meatloaf with your hands making it look like a loaf of bread.

Cook for 30 minutes and garnish the top with the barbecue sauce and the seeds. Cook for another 5 minutes and then cool for 15 minutes before serving.

22. Tuscan Keto Chicken

Tuscan flavor is not just for taste, but a lifestyle based on Tuscany, Italy. Here food and culture meet in a climatic medley of culture. Try this chicken and be whisked away . . .

Ingredients:

- ✓ 2 pounds boneless skinless chicken breasts, thinly sliced

- ✓ ½ lime fresh squeezed

- ✓ /12 teaspoon chili powder

- ✓ 2 tablespoons olive oil

- ✓ 1 tablespoon sunflower oil OR coconut oil

- ✓ 1 cup heavy cream

- ✓ ½ cup chicken broth

- ✓ 2 cloves of garlic minced

- ✓ 2 teaspoons Italian seasoning

- ✓ ½ cup parmesan cheese

- ✓ 1 cup fresh spinach leaves

✓ ½ cup sun dried tomatoes

Directions:

In a medium mixing bowl, place the chicken and lime with the chili powder and the sunflower or coconut oil. Stir until well coated.

Preheat oven to 360 degrees.

In a Pyrex baking dish or lasagna pan, place chicken strips on the bottom with the remnants from the mixing bowl over the chicken.

In the same mixing bowl add the remaining ingredients (everything else) and mix for about 30 beats with a wooden spoon. Pour / scrape everything and cover the chicken. Bake for 15 minutes, turn the chicken and bake for another 15 minutes. Serve immediately.

23. Keto Shrimp Alfredo

If you love shrimp Alfredo and still want to live the Keto lifestyle, you have to try this recipe. Simply mix the ingredients together and bake.

Ingredients:

- ✓ 2 pounds raw peeled shrimp (buy from local farms not China)

- ✓ 2 tablespoons natural butter

- ✓ ½ white onion diced

- ✓ 1 small packet cream cheese at room temperature

- ✓ 1 cup heavy cream

- ✓ ¼ cup whole milk

- ✓ 2 cloves of garlic minced

- ✓ 1 teaspoon basil

- ✓ 1 teaspoon salt

- ✓ ½ cup shredded Parmesan cheese

- ✓ ¼ cup olives, diced

- ✓ ½ tablespoon olive oil

- ✓ 2 sun dried tomatoes diced

- ✓ 1 cup baby spinach, fresh

Directions:

In a large skillet, add the shrimp, butter, salt and garlic. Cook for about 3 minutes on a medium heat, stirring occasionally. Next add the remaining ingredients except for the spinach. Stir often, folding until all ingredients are incorporated and a nice and savory white Alfredo sauce appears. Cook for about 5 minutes or less. Do NOT overcook or you will burn the sauce.

When the consistency runs like thick maple syrup, it should be ready and since you pre-cooked the shrimp, the flavors will complement the final dish with the shrimp cooked correctly.

24. Bacon Eggplant Alfredo

Eggplant can be made quite tasty with bacon and Alfredo sauce. If you need a different dish, here is one that is sure to please even family and friends.

Ingredients:

- ✓ 1-pound bacon

- ✓ 2 pounds eggplant, pre-cooked and cubed

- ✓ 1 tablespoon coconut oil

- ✓ 1 tablespoon olive oil

- ✓ 1 cup heavy cream

- ✓ 2 tablespoons natural butter

- ✓ 2 cloves garlic minced

- ✓ 1 tablespoon white wine (optional but it helps the taste)

- ✓ 1 tablespoon lemon juice

- ✓ 1 cup shredded Parmesan cheese

Directions:

Preheat oven to 350.

Add all oils to the bottom of the cooking dish with the coconut oil and olive oil drizzled over the eggplant.

Next add all the remaining ingredients into a mixing bowl and stir for about a minute until a smooth consistency.

Pour the mixing bowl contents over the eggplant. Cook for 30 minutes; remove and let cool for about 15 minutes. You can serve immediately or reheat later. The taste actually improves over time . . .

25. Zucchini & Almond Pesto

Pesto is a great way to experience foods that are well ground and easy to digest. You can eat it straight or on low carb wraps / chips. You can also add it to other meals as a sauce or flavor enhancer.

Ingredients:

- ✓ 2 medium Zucchinis cut into cubes

- ✓ 1 avocado, cut, peeled & cubed

- ✓ ¼ cup walnuts

- ✓ ¼ cup fresh basil leaves

- ✓ ¼ cup almond slices

- ✓ 2 cloves garlic peeled

- ✓ ½ peeled lemon OR juiced

- ✓ ¼ cup grated Parmesan cheese

- ✓ 1 tablespoon olive oil

- ✓ ½ tablespoon Italian seasoning

- ✓ 1 pinch of Salt and pepper

Directions:

This recipe is easy to make. Simply place all of the ingredients in a food processor and grind until you have a smooth paste, about 30-45 seconds.

The pesto can be eaten cold like a dip.

You can add the pesto to other recipes for flavor and food enhancement. For example, baked chicken with the pesto on top.

I also suggest trying this pesto with Keto bread or low carb tort chips. Finally, you can add the pesto to wraps with meat like lamb or chicken for a quick meal.

26. Macho Nachos With Steak & Cheeses

Nachos? Yes, you can have nachos if you use this recipe. Here's how to make your own like this.

Ingredients:

- ✓ 1-pound beef round tip steak
- ✓ 2 tablespoons natural butter
- ✓ ½ white onions minced
- ✓ 1 teaspoon chili powder

The "chips:"

- ✓ 2 medium torts
- ✓ 2 tablespoons of coconut oil
- ✓ ½ teaspoon turmeric

The Nacho Toppings:

- ✓ 1-pound cauliflower cooked & shredded
- ✓ ½ cup shredded cheddar cheese
- ✓ ½ cup shredded Monterey jack

- ✓ ½ cup sour cream

- ✓ ½ mashed avocado

- ✓ 2 tablespoons coconut oil

Directions:

In a large skillet, add the chips ingredients and cook until they begin to harden like regular chips, about 3 minutes on high flame. Remove.

Now add main steak ingredients and cook for several minutes on a high flame, mixing often and then remove. Repeat the process for macho toppings and assemble everything together like classic nachos. Enjoy!

27. Chicken Skillet With Honey & Walnuts

This recipe is actually quite easy to make. Finally, here is a fantastic Keto recipe that is skillet based and sweet. With healthy fats and real honey, the flavor makes all the difference to your Keto lifestyle.

Ingredients:

- ✓ 2 chicken breasts cut into long strips

- ✓ 2 tablespoons of coconut oil

- ✓ 1 green pepper diced

- ✓ 1 tablespoon local honey

- ✓ ½ cup walnuts

- ✓ ½ teaspoon paprika

- ✓ 2 scallions diced

Salad:

- ✓ 2 cups thin chopped romaine

- ✓ 1 tablespoon ranch

- ✓ 1 tablespoon salad oil

- ✓ ½ tablespoon white vinegar or vinaigrette

- ✓ ½ tablespoon walnuts

- ✓ ½ tablespoon flax seeds

- ✓ 2-5 cherry tomatoes

Directions:

In a medium skillet, place all of the first set of ingredients and cook on a medium heat for about 5 minutes stirring occasionally. Plate up salad and add chicken and enjoy!

28. Sweet N' Sour Keto Meatballs

These meatballs will add some sweet and sassy taste to any dinner table. Only you will know they are for your new Keto lifestyle, so cook them up and enjoy.

Ingredients:

The meatballs

- ✓ 1-pound ground beef

- ✓ 1 egg, whisked in a cup with a dash of salt and pepper

- ✓ ½ white onion minced

- ✓ ¼ cup Parmesan cheese

- ✓ ½ teaspoon garlic powder

- ✓ 1 teaspoon Worcestershire sauce

For the sauce

- ✓ 1 ½ cups water

- ✓ ¼ cup apple cider vinegar

- ✓ 3 tablespoons soy sauce

- ✓ ½ cup sugar free ketchup

- ✓ ½ teaspoon Stevia

Directions:

Let meat stand out of the refrigerator for about 1 hour to warm it up for ease of handling. Preheat oven to 350 degrees. In a mixing bowl add all of the meatball ingredients and mix with your hand. Form into golf ball sizes and place on cookie sheet.

For the sauce: simply mix it all together and whisk it for about 30 strokes. In a small saucepan, heat sauce for about 5 minutes on low heat. Pour over meatballs and serve when done.

29. Keto Gyros With Ranch & Feta Cheese

Gyros can be a great dinner or a quick lunch too. They have delicious flavor and with the right combination of herbs, you too will be having them more and more.

Ingredients:

Gyro Meat

✓ 1-pound ground lamb

✓ 1 cup pork rinds or pigs ears

✓ 2 tablespoons coconut oil

✓ 1 cup feta cheese

✓ Himalayan salt & pepper to taste

✓ 1 tablespoon oregano

✓ 3 cloves garlic minced

Gyro Sauce and torts

✓ ½ cup low carb ranch

✓ 1 tablespoon coconut oil

- ✓ 1 tablespoon white vinegar

- ✓ 2 tablespoons olive oil

- ✓ ½ cup diced cucumbers, 4-6 flour torts, low carb or coconut

- ✓ 2 cups thin sliced in strips, romaine lettuce

Directions:

Use low carb wraps or coconut flour wraps. In a mixing bowl combine all of the gyro meat ingredients and hand mix thoroughly. Make into flat patties and cook in a skillet like hamburgers.

Combine all sauce ingredients and mix. Assemble gyros with cubed meat and pour sauce and add romaine lettuce. Enjoy!

30. Italian Sausage Skillet Bake With Salsa

This simple skillet meal is a snap to make and it is also a great dinner meal to make when time is short.

Ingredients:

- ✓ 4 Italian sausages diced OR Keto sausages (see recipe 3 in breakfast)

- ✓ 3 tablespoons Dijon mustard

- ✓ 2 garlic cloves minced

- ✓ 2 tablespoons coconut oil

Remaining Ingredients

- ✓ ½ cup heavy whipping cream

- ✓ ½ cup tomato sauce

- ✓ ½ cup water

- ✓ Dash Himalayan salt and white pepper

- ✓ 1 cup fresh spinach leaves

- ✓ ½ cup grated Parmesan cheese

✓ 1 teaspoon parsley flakes

✓ 1 cup shredded sharp cheese

✓ 1 cup mild (or hot) salsa

Directions:

In a medium skillet: add sausages, mustard, garlic and coconut oil. Cook on a medium heat for several minutes then add the water and tomato paste.

Next add all remaining ingredients except the whipping cream. Cook for another few minutes on a medium flame and finally add the whipping cream and fold for about 1 minute. If you like it hot, add a dash of tabasco sauce. Serve immediately.

31. Skillet Chicken With Tasty Greens & Cheddar Sauce

This final recipe is also a skillet meal and is a great way to substitute from mac n' cheese. The chicken makes the dish really work well.

Ingredients:

- ✓ 1-pound boneless chicken breasts cut into strips

- ✓ 2 tablespoons coconut oil

- ✓ 1 tablespoon Italian dressing

The Veggies & Spices

- ✓ 1 cup chicken stock

- ✓ 1 cup heavy cream

- ✓ 2 cups dark leafy baby spinach leaves

- ✓ 1 green pepper, diced

- ✓ 1 tablespoon diced chives

- ✓ 1 tablespoon olive oil

- ✓ 2 tablespoons coconut flour

- ✓ ½ teaspoon white pepper

- ✓ Dash Himalayan salt

Directions:

In a medium skillet, add the first set of ingredients (chicken) and cook for about 5 minutes on a medium flame. Set aside for a moment.

In a medium mixing bowl, add all remaining ingredients. Stir for a minute and then empty bowl into the skillet.

Cook for another 3 minutes on a medium heat mixing occasionally. Serve immediately.

Keto Snacks Bonus Section

Snack yourself to health? Yes!

These snacks are great for life on the fly. Now you can pass temptation when you make these snack foods and take them with you.

Not only are these snacks are designed to be tasty, but finally you will have real choices to keep and maintain your Keto Lifestyle.

We also incorporated "superfoods" as part of these snacks so that the nutrition and healthiness is there. Never skip a meal again and use foods like this to maintain your Keto lifestyle.

1. Keto Vanilla Or Chocolate Rich & Creamy Shake

This is a simple way to have a meal replacement and enjoy either a chocolate or vanilla treat.

Ingredients:

- ✓ 2 scoops high quality chocolate or vanilla ice cream

- ✓ 1 tablespoon cocoa or vanilla powder

- ✓ 2 tablespoons coconut oil

- ✓ 1 tablespoon unsweetened chocolate or vanilla shavings

- ✓ 1 tablespoon of heavy cream

- ✓ 1 tablespoon coconut shavings

- ✓ ½ cup blueberries or raspberries

Directions:

Place all ingredients into a blender and blend until rich and creamy.

Variants:

Some people add two raw eggs and blend as well. You can also add liquid supplements to your morning shake such as vitamins.

If you want a tang to your shakes, add the juice of an orange and you have what is essentially an orange Julius™ but this will spike sugar.

I suggest using lime as this adds alkaline properties as well as vitamin C without the sugar. If you love orange use orange spice or orange zest and Stevia as a reasonable substitute.

Finally, lemon and lime are great additives with Stevia as well.

2. Pork Rinds Mix With Nuts

This simple snack includes superfoods (nuts) if you follow this easy mix. This is also good trail mix and can help keep you going throughout the day:

Ingredients:

- ✓ 1 cup pork rinds

- ✓ ½ cup dried fruit of choice (low glycemic)

- ✓ ½ cup almonds

- ✓ ½ cup almond slivers

- ✓ ½ cup sunflower seeds

- ✓ ½ cup chia seeds

- ✓ ½ cup flaxseeds

- ✓ ½ cup pumpkin seeds

Directions:

Thoroughly mix all ingredients in a medium mixing bowl and add to zip lock bags.

The snack is perfect for on the fly because it does not need refrigeration and will help you curb hunger and temptation.

Do NOT buy seeds that are processed with salt or sugar and always favor seeds that have their skins intact wherever possible.

Other variants include adding coconut oil and baking the mix into bars that can then be eaten like a snack bar:

To Make A Snack Bar: add two tablespoons of coconut oil, 1 egg and1/2 tablespoon coconut flour. Mix, place in a small pan and cook at 350 for 15 minutes. Cut and refrigerate and serve as snack bar.

3. Dark Chocolate & Crunchy Seed Bar

If you liked the last recipe, you are going to love this one. Here we make a mix that we bake and cut into delicious and sweet tasting chocolate. Not only is this extremely healthy, but there is no actual sugar and tons of protein.

Ingredients:

- ✓ ½ cup dark chocolate or similar unsweetened cocoa

- ✓ 1 egg, whisked with a pinch of Himalayan salt

- ✓ 1 teaspoon Stevia

- ✓ 2 tablespoons of natural butter

- ✓ 2 tablespoons of coconut oil

- ✓ 2 tablespoons coconut oil to grease a pan

- ✓ ½ cup coconut flour

- ✓ ½ cup dried fruit of choice (low glycemic)

- ✓ ½ cup almonds

- ✓ ½ cup almond slivers

- ✓ ½ cup sunflower seeds

- ✓ ½ cup chia seeds

- ✓ ½ cup flaxseeds

- ✓ ½ cup pumpkin seeds

Directions:

Place all ingredients in a medium mixing bowl and hand mix with a wooden spoon about 30 beats.

Preheat oven to 350 degrees. In a coconut greased pan, add the mix and bake for 15 minutes. Let cool for 1 hour and then cut into bars. Try these as meal replacements or for snacks.

4. Dark Chocolate "Pudding" A La Avocado

Avocados make excellent pudding and when seasoned carefully they are almost indistinguishable from real carb laden puddings. Avocados are an excellent source of healthy fats and there is no baking involved.

Ingredients:

- ✓ 1 large avocado peeled and cubed
- ✓ ½ cup dark baking chocolate, unsweetened
- ✓ ½ tablespoon cocoa
- ✓ 1 teaspoon Stevia
- ✓ ½ teaspoon vanilla extract
- ✓ 1 tablespoon heavy cream
- ✓ 1 dash cinnamon
- ✓ 1 dash salt
- ✓ 1 dash nutmeg

Directions:

In a medium mixing bowl, mash the avocado and then mix all the remaining ingredients together, first with a wooden spoon and then finish with a hand mixer. You can serve immediately.

Whipped topping:

- ✓ 1 cup heavy whipping cream

- ✓ 1 teaspoon vanilla

- ✓ 1 teaspoon Stevia

Mix on high until it's whipped cream consistency. Add to pudding.

5. Peanut Butter & Chocolate Bars With Almonds

Inspired by several popular candy bars, here is a healthy variant you can easily make, mix and bake. Once done serve and you won't believe these are sugar free and almost carb free.

Ingredients:

- ✓ ½ cup organic peanut butter

- ✓ ½ cup baking chocolate unsweetened

- ✓ 1 tablespoon cocoa

- ✓ 1 teaspoon vanilla extract

- ✓ 1 teaspoon Stevia

- ✓ 1 egg

- ✓ ½ cup coconut flour

- ✓ 2 tablespoons natural butter

- ✓ 1 tablespoon coconut oil

- ✓ 2 tablespoons coconut oil to grease the pan

- ✓ ½ cup almonds

Directions:

In a medium mixing bowl, add all ingredients and beat with a spoon until all ingredients look reasonably incorporated.

If necessary add a few pinches more of coconut flour until a thick consistency that will still run like pancake batter.

Preheat oven to 350 and in a greased small lasagna pan or pyrex dish, cook for 15 minutes.

6. Kale Chips With Barbecue Seasoning

Making kale chips is easy and just requires a few minutes. You will be surprised at how good these are and with different seasoning you can change the flavor easily.

Ingredients:

- ✓ 1 bunch kale

- ✓ 2 tablespoons olive oil

- ✓ 2 tablespoon Parmesan cheese

- ✓ 1 tablespoon garlic powder

- ✓ 1 teaspoon of Himalayan salt

- ✓ 1 tablespoon barbecue seasoning

Directions:

Wash the kale and pick out leaves and snip with scissors to shape on rounds.

In a mixing bowl add all the ingredients and the shaped chips. Toss like a salad coating the chips with the ingredients.

Preheat oven to 300 degrees.

On a cookie sheet place chips and cook for 15 minutes, turning the chips once during the process.

Remember you can season these chips by using almost any combination of spices so experiment and see what you can concoct.

You can also just use larger leaves for a bigger chip.

7. Keto Brownies With Nuts

If you like brownies but can't have the sugar, try these. Unlike typical brownies they are healthy, yet still have a consistency and taste of decadent chocolate.

Ingredients:

- ✓ 1 avocado peeled and cubed

- ✓ ½ cup of coconut oil

- ✓ 2 tablespoons of coconut oil (grease the pan)

- ✓ ½ cup cocoa

- ✓ 2 tablespoons natural butter

- ✓ ½ cup coconut flour

- ✓ ½ teaspoon baking powder

- ✓ 1 teaspoon Stevia

- ✓ ½ cup dark baking chocolate

- ✓ 2 eggs, whisked with a dash of salt

- ✓ ½ teaspoon vanilla extract

✓ ½ cup almond slivers or walnuts

Directions:

In a medium mixing bowl, add the avocado and mash first. Now add the rest of the ingredients and beat with a hand mixer on medium for about 2 minutes. Preheat oven to 350 degrees.

In a brownie pan, add coconut oil to grease the pan. Next pour the brownie mix and use a spatula to smooth it into the pan. Bake for 15 minutes and let cool for 1 hour before eating.

If you want to add a topping, use 1 cup heavy whipping cream, 1 teaspoon vanilla and 1 teaspoon Stevia to a cold bowl.

Mix on high until whipped cream consistency. Add to brownies.

8. Cucumber Boats With Cream Cheese & Raspberries

This simple recipe will actually surprise you because it tastes decadent but is really a tasty snack that is filling:

Ingredients:

- ✓ 2 medium cucumbers, cut in half and carefully peeled

- ✓ 1 package of Philly cream cheese

- ✓ 1 pinch of salt per cucumber

- ✓ ½ cup whipping cream

- ✓ 1 dash of Stevia

- ✓ The Raspberry filling:

- ✓ ½ cup raspberries, strained through a collander, no seeds

- ✓ ¼ cup water, warm

- ✓ 1 teaspoon Stevia

- ✓ 1 pinch of cinnamon

✓ 1 teaspoon of Jello mix, red

Directions:

Using a spoon dig out a "trench" so that the cucumber boat will be formed and maximize what it can hold. Add the remnants of the cucumber to a mixing bowl and combine all of the first ingredients.

In a second mixing bowl combine all the raspberry topping mix. Blend and then add to the first set of ingredients and mix by hand again.

Now spoon the filling into the cucumber boats and serve.

.

9. Quick Vanilla White Chocolate Cupcakes

These are essentially mix, pour and bake and eat. Can't get much simpler and you will still be 100% on track for your new Keto Lifestyle.

Ingredients:

- ✓ ½ cup unsweetened white chocolate
- ✓ ½ cup coconut flour
- ✓ ¼ cup coconut oil
- ✓ 2 tablespoons coconut oil for cupcake wells
- ✓ 1 teaspoon Stevia
- ✓ 3 tablespoons coconut flour
- ✓ 1 teaspoon vanilla extract
- ✓ ½ teaspoon baking powder
- ✓ 1 scoop good quality vanilla protein powder
- ✓ 1 egg

Directions:

In a mixing bowl combine all the ingredients and beat with a hand mixer on high for 1 minute.

Preheat oven to 350 degrees.

In a cupcake tray, grease each well with coconut oil and pour the batter about half way into each well.

Cook for 15 minutes and let stand for 30 minutes to cool.

You can add almond slivers for additional taste and garnish.

Conclusion

Wow! What an amazing cooking journey we have had together!

As you can see, we have covered lots of great recipes that are not only tasty, but filled with nutrition and flavor.

It was my goal to also give you a set of core ingredients so that as you cooked, you began to see how many of these ingredients are used again and again.

This helps you not only learn how to cook, but to simplify your life and raise your skills, -- as well as make your shopping list much easier when it comes time to get what you need for cooking.

Remember that you need to keep the fat content up in these recipes so follow the directions carefully.

If a recipe does not call for many additional fats, this is because it can be found in the food itself, like the brownie recipe with avocados as a main ingredient.

I hope you learned a lot about Keto cooking here. I promise you if you follow these recipes you will love the foods and grow healthier as long as you always purchase the best organic components for each recipe.

You should also experiment with your own recipes using core cooking principles you have learned in this cookbook.

You will find that over time, you will become quite skilled with cooking these dishes and you will hardly need to consult the recipes because this book was laid out that way for overlapping cooking knowledge.

But Wait...Before you move ahead, I have good news for you. This book offers you a **FREE BONUS "35 Tips To GO LOW CARB When Eating Out ($19 Value)"**.

You can access your free report by visiting the below URL.

http://geni.us/freeketorecipes

Best Regards,
David F. Wilson

Made in the USA
Middletown, DE
30 July 2019